FEAR NOT:
A CHRISTIAN VIEW
OF DEATH

FEAR NOT:
A CHRISTIAN VIEW OF DEATH

Manford G. Gutzke

BAKER BOOK HOUSE
Grand Rapids, Michigan

Contents

1
Introduction

Have you ever wondered why people do not want to face death? "And as it is appointed unto men once to die, but after this the judgment. . . ." These words are found in Hebrews 9:27.

In this series of studies we shall be thinking about death, particularly asking and answering this question: What does the Bible say about death? This will be our intent, to find out the Biblical view of death.

No one has to prove the reality of death. We not only see it around us but we feel it in our bones. The day will come when we will have to leave this world. Death is universal; it comes to everyone. It comes to the good and it comes to the bad. It comes to the old and it comes to the young. Why should anyone want to avoid mention or discussion of death? I am not going to criticize or scold anybody about that, but I am interested. Why should I feel myself shrinking back whenever death is mentioned?

Living in this world is like a journey into the unknown. Each day is new. Each night brings the curtain down to end one more day that will never be repeated. In time we become familiar with the dawn, the clouds, the sunshine, and the rain; but we never know for sure what to expect even of the weather. We get to know people. We fear that we may have enemies. We cherish loved ones. Yet the desire to live is universal. Even for those who live in tragic hopelessness, living is still desirable. The will to live is in every creature no matter how much the trouble, how sharp the pain, how dreary the outlook, or how difficult the problem.

Not long ago I remember talking to a woman who was dying. Every aspect of her lovely home showed the touch of her thoughtful, artistic hand. Her husband was a good man — successful in business, faithful in his home, which evidenced refinement and affluence. It was obvious that this woman had everything to live for. I do not think that she was fifty years of age, but she was dying. She believed in the Lord and had tried to be a true witness to Jesus Christ. She trusted in God and had tried to be faithful. I told her of God's plan to bring her to Himself. She had not been a wicked person and had no keen sense of sin. Forgiveness was good, but it was not precious to her because she had not really, in her own estimation I am sure, felt very much need for the mercy of God. She had no reason to wish for anything else than what she already had. She had not promoted her fellowship with the Lord here on earth; so she had no great joy in the prospect of being with Him forever. The thought of going to heaven did not especially appeal to her. In fact, I was not sure that she had given it much attention. To her, the idea of dying was bleak — she would be leaving so much with regret, to enter into something about which she had so little hope. My heart went out to her in sympathy. She was the unfortunate victim of a faulty view of living. Man is made so that he can recognize and appreciate the blessings of heaven while he is in this world — but she had missed that.

Men have held various attitudes toward death. There is no way to feel satisfied about it. For some, as in the case of the woman I have mentioned, death is an unwelcome interruption of a satisfying and challenging experience here on earth. For others, whose daily life is an unending burden, death is a blessed relief. But there always is the element of tragedy, the inevitable break off from all that is familiar, and the blind plunge into the dark unknown. It is no wonder that many fear death. Some fear because of their conscience. They dread meeting the holy God as Judge. Though they actually live in His presence every day and all they have ever done or are doing now is known to God like an open book, it is still true that as long as they are not reconciled to Him through Jesus Christ they shrink from meeting Him face to face.

Poets have romanticized death. Some speak of it as the Great Adventure, but others call it the Grim Reaper. There is no way to deny its reality and its effect. Death is the great leveler, because in death no one is preferred. No one is great. No one is small. Facing death, no one is strong and no one is weak. No one is wise and no one is good. Always, there is one common aspect about death: it is final. Death has the last word.

Usually we think of death as the appropriate ending of a long day. Some of us have looked upon the still face of a child lying in death, and it was hard to accept. Sometimes death comes as the conclusion of a long illness. Sometimes it comes as a result of a violent calamity, and, sometimes, after long, unbearable pain. Sometimes death comes in sleep; but always it comes. Each of us will meet it. It is as common as mankind. It is a great joy, for those of us who believe, to be reminded that Christ Jesus came to abolish death and to bring life and immortality to light through the gospel. He gained the victory over death, and for all believers death has lost its sting.

As we think on these things we are going to be bringing this to our minds. We are going to be remembering that although death is absolutely unavoidable and we all are moving toward it, it is the exit from this world. It is the only exit. This is the way all of us are going. But Christ Jesus went through it, and He fixed it in such a way that in the Lord, death for us has lost its sting. There is no longer a need for us to fear death.

The Bible gives the most eloquent description of death in all of literature:

Remember now thy Creator in the days of thy youth, while the evil days come not, nor the years draw nigh, when thou shalt say, I have no pleasure in them; while the sun, or the light, or the moon, or the stars, be not darkened, nor the clouds return after the rain: in the day when the keepers of the house shall tremble, and the strong men shall bow themselves, and the grinders cease because they are few, and those that look out of the windows be darkened, and the doors shall be shut in the streets, when the sound of the grinding is low, and he shall rise up at the voice of the bird, and all the daughters of music shall be brought low; also when they shall be afraid of that which is high, and fears shall be in the way, and the almond tree shall flourish, and the grasshopper shall be a burden, and desire shall fail: because man goeth to his long home, and the mourners go about the streets: or ever the silver cord be loosed, or the golden bowl be broken, or the pitcher be broken at the fountain, or the wheel broken at the cistern. Then shall the dust return to the earth as it was: and the spirit shall return unto God who gave it (Eccles. 12:1-7).

2
Death
Is the
Consequence of Sin

Have you ever wondered about the reason for death in this world? Why is there death?

The Bible gives us a very simple explanation. Paul writes: "For the wages of sin is death; but the gift of God is eternal life through Jesus Christ our Lord" (Rom. 6:23). In this passage there is a significant distinction indicated between "wages" and "a gift." Something was done to earn the wages of sin: sin has earned it. But a gift is something to be received. It is free. The gift of God is eternal life through our Lord Jesus Christ. The story of the creation and fall of man as told in Genesis can well be taken to show that God intended for man to enjoy blessedness with God. But there is still much we do not know. Why would God make man as he is, knowing that man would sin? Why did God create the world as it is, knowing that eventually He would destroy it? We do not know. But the facts of life are as they are, not as we think they should be.

Living goes on in interchange with the environment. It is not fixed in any one pattern. It is not stereotyped. It is possible to live in such a way that living brings joy, and it also is possible to live so that we bring distress to ourselves and others. Man can and must select in this world what he will have for himself. Man is surrounded by all manner of things, and he has the opportunity to select whatever he will take for himself, some of which will be helpful and some, hurtful. There is both food and poison within man's reach. This world offers both. It is vital that a man chooses that which will be helpful; but it is fatal for man to choose that which will be hurtful.

God is in the world. When we think about man dealing with the world we must also think about man dealing with God. I do not know how so many people get the idea they can handle the world as it is and leave God out. Nonetheless, the world is in the hands of God, and when a man looks out on the world he not only thinks about the earth, water, sky, air, trees, and animals, but he thinks about God who is there, too. Man's life depends on how he handles the things of this world — the good and the bad, and above all else, how he will deal with God, his Maker, Keeper, and Judge. More than anything else, man must respond to the reality of God to be blessed.

God is a living Being with a personal interest in each creature. He has made the world as it is; and He has made man as he is, knowing that man moves over a strange road, facing an indefinite variety of alternatives with unknown potentials for good and for evil. God is available to man and willing to guide him along the way so that he may find blessing. It is of utmost importance that man respond to God in obedience, that he might have the benefit of His guidance in living so that he might be blessed. This leads us to say that to ignore God or to disobey God is sin. It sounds so simple — just three little letters — s-i-n. Sin is anything contrary to the will of God, anything that is different from God.

We have light as opposed to darkness; straight as opposed to crooked; success as opposed to failure, and good as opposed to bad. We have obedience as opposed to sin. It has been the sad state of man that as he faced the possibilities in living he chose to please himself. Thus he disobeyed the will of God. Such transgression was sin, and this brought to man the consequence about which he had been warned: "the wages of sin is death." Because of sin, death came upon all.

> Therefore as by the offence of one judgment came upon all men to condemnation; even so by the righteousness of one the free gift came upon all men unto justification of life (Rom. 5:18).

I am sure you recognize right away that the "offence of one" was the sin of Adam and even so, "by the righteousness of one" — Jesus of Nazareth — the free gift came upon all men unto justification of life.

> For as by one man's disobedience many were made sinners, so by the obedience of one shall many be made righteous. Moreover the law entered, that the offence might abound. But where sin abounded, grace did much more abound: that as sin hath reigned unto death, even so might grace reign through righteousness unto eternal life of Jesus Christ our Lord (Rom. 5:19-21).

The natural man may feel justified in saying, "I don't deserve to die." The believing man could say, "I don't deserve to live forever." It would be true in each case, but there is something very important here for us to keep in mind: death is not punishment as such. It isn't something added to the whole situation. It is the consequence of Adam's conduct. When he did what he wanted to do he was starting the process that would take him away from God, the source of life, and death is the condition of not having life. Furthermore, eternal life is not a reward. We may refer to it in that fashion, but it is a consequence of what Christ has done. Christ Jesus died for us and rose from the dead, and we, too, can be raised from the dead.

Keep this clear in your mind. You may never have personally accepted Jesus Christ as your Savior, but let me ask this question: Do you think it is wise for you to go on the rest of your life without Him? He came to this world for you. He died for you. This is God's plan for you. God does not have a plan for you to live on your own. God's entire situation is set up in such a way that if you stay on your own, death and destruction will surely come to you. But you can be saved. Christ Jesus died for that very reason, and eternal life will be the consequence of what Christ has done.

Why is it like that? I don't know. I can't explain to you why God has arranged it that way. But I can tell you one thing: we can join in thanking God for His grace and mercy. Believe me, although it is true that death is the consequence of sin, we can thank God that eternal life is the free gift through our Lord Jesus Christ.

3
Fear of Death
Is
Bondage

Do you know why the fear of death is so common to the human heart?

In Hebrews 2:14-15 we read about the Lord Jesus Christ:

Forasmuch then as the children are partakers of flesh and blood, he also himself likewise took part of the same; that through death he might destroy him that had the power of death, that is, the devil; and deliver them who through fear of death were all their lifetime subject to bondage.

It is natural for a human being to fear death. Different persons may have different thoughts and they may dress it up in different ways and I know some poets have done a wonderful work in making aspects of death more acceptable to us, but the prospect of dying is sobering. For some it is a threatening experience. If that should be the case with you, you are not unusual. Your experience is normal. It is proper. It is not so much the actual experience of dying that need bother a person so much, but what comes afterwards.

Our whole sense of apprehension, and by that I mean the fear of death, is grounded in our basic belief in the hereafter. In spite of what anybody may say, one of the reasons why a person shrinks back from death is because after death comes the judgment. It is bad enough that death interrupts what is going on, that death breaks off everything I have here. I must leave so much undone. And what next? What happens after death? Fear of the unknown is a common human experience. I can remember on one occasion when a grandson, who was perhaps four years old, was with me while I was splitting wood for the fireplace. A large area in our backyard was cleared, where I was working with the wood. Back of that there were tall trees and a dark valley. The child played around for fifteen or twenty minutes while dusk was settling. Then I noticed how, as it grew darker, he stayed closer to me. That was very natural, common conduct.

We are always uneasy about a new road. Here we have to be on the lookout. Even in such a thing as being on a new job, we must be alert and on the lookout. We cannot go with the same feeling of familiarity and lack of worry, as we would on an old job. In every new job there is always something we could call fear; at least it is a feeling of concern. This fear of the unknown is part of the fear of death. There is no human way of knowing what goes on on the other side—and you and I are going there. Also, there is a dread of anything that is final. It is bad enough to have something happen that is not good, something that is hard, but if there is the expectation that it may soon be over and that one of these days we will have it better it can be borne. But death is final. It is finished. That is all. And that is what we mean by death. There can be no commutation of the sentence of death.

As believing people we know there is something good after death; but may I say kindly, so far as the whole world is concerned we are the only people who do know. We believe in the One who went through death, and came out on the other side alive. In Him we expect to have that happen to us. But so far as death itself is concerned from a human point of view, we realize we can't change the fact of it disrupting our plans, breaking off human relationships.

After death there is no more opportunity, no chance to do differently, but only the judgment. It is bad enough so far as this world is concerned that everything is broken off, but after death we come into the presence of One who knows us altogether. There we can expect to see our unfinished business. We shrink back to think of how many things there will be that we have not done. That will be harvest time, and in a very real and sobering sense, the moment of truth. That will be the exposure of our life as it is; it will be meeting the Judge.

This is the unhappy, tragic outlook for the unbeliever and we should not blame him for being concerned and not wanting to think about it. There is a fear of death that is bondage to the soul. But this need not be the lot of any man. I rejoice to remember the fellowship I have had with souls who were free from the bondage of death.

I remember one dear lady in my first congregation. She had a heart condition that affected her in such a way there was a common understanding among us in the church that she could pass away any time. She was confined to her home. I often visited her and was always impressed with her serenity. She was unafraid. One day I asked her to tell me how it was that she could be so in her condition. She replied, "I have never been to heaven, and I have never been to the world after this one. But I had not been to this world either when I first came. My God who created me and caused me to be born fixed it so that there were people to care for me. I was helpless. But loving hands cared for me and enabled me to live in this world. The same God will be over there, and when I go over there I have the feeling that if He arranged for people to care for me here, He will arrange to take care of me there. And besides, my Lord will be there and I know about Him. He died for me. So what have I to be worried about?" Oh, how I wished every member of my church could have that serene outlook about the future. Why did she have it? She was free because of her faith in God, her faith in the Lord.

I think again of the first time I was present at a deathbed. As a new minister of the gospel, before I was ordained to preach, I was a student pulpit supply in a church. A woman who was about forty years of age was stricken suddenly with an infection in her blood which took her life in a matter of a couple of days. I saw her on the last day she was alive. She knew she was going to die. I could not understand how she could be so peaceful. I asked her if she realized what was going to happen and she said, "Do you mean, why am I not afraid? You taught me to say, 'The Lord is my shepherd. I shall not want.'" She went through the twenty-third Psalm and when she quoted, "Yea though I walk through the valley of the shadow of death, I will fear no evil . . . " she smiled into my face. I wished right then that I could meet all of the skeptics and the agnostics in the world. I would have liked to tell them something—that a person who believes in the Lord can actually pass out of this world without any fear, trusting in Him.

Remember that passage in Isaiah 41:13, "For I the

Lord thy God will hold thy right hand, saying unto thee, Fear not; I will help thee."

4
Death
Is
Unavoidable

Can you see that one of the awful facts about death is that you cannot avoid it?

We now turn in the Scriptures to the Old Testament where we find an incident that brings one aspect of this whole matter of death to light. In Genesis is the record of the incident where Hagar had been sent out from Abraham's house with her son. As you know, they wandered in the desert until they were almost dead.

And the water was spent in the bottle, and she cast the child under one of the shrubs. And she went, and sat her down over against him a good way off, as it were a bowshot: for she said, Let me not see the death of the child. And she sat over against him, and lift up her voice, and wept (Gen. 21:15-16).

I am sure that every person who understands that situation would thoroughly sympathize with Hagar. Her grief and despair can be appreciated by anybody. She was helpless. This same situation may account for the tragic sadness in the heart of so many people. So much in life is beyond our control.

The world is as it is; we cannot change it. My heritage is what it is. Consider your family, you had nothing to do with that. It is the same with your culture: you did not make it; it was here when you came. Even your language you learned from other people. Your values were inculcated from other people. The community where you live has a great significance in your life, but you had very little to do with it. The social group that you belong to influences you to a great extent. What happened to you yesterday, the day before, last week, a month ago, a year ago, five years ago: all your life your experiences are what they are; you cannot change them now. As they were occurring you might have thought you could do this or that; but when they once were done, they were done and you were the one who, as it were, reaped the result. Even Providence is what it is. You did not have anything to do with that as things happened, and there is very little anybody can do about it all now.

In the course of my whole life there seems to have been two great decisive days in my life. One of them is my birth. Certainly everybody would admit that was very important. The other will be the day of my death. That will also be very important. These are the beginning and the ending. Is not death like the coming of the night? It cannot be stopped. The sun will set regardless. Since we cannot prevent death, then what can we do? The Bible tells us something about what we can do. We are given instructions all the way through the Bible how to live and how to die. It is true we cannot avoid death, but I will tell you one thing: we can get ready for it. We can prepare. "So teach us to number our days, that we may apply our hearts unto wisdom" (Ps. 90:12). Sooner or later a man will die, so far as this world is concerned. Then he will stand in the presence of his God. Any man who realizes this is a wise man.

Then what shall we say to each other and what does the Bible say about this inevitable event? Let us get ready. If I knew that Sunday night would be my last day to live, what would I want to do? To begin with there are some things I would like to finish. Some things I am doing right now I would want to hurry up and get finished. I would hate to leave them where they are. Then there are things I have always meant to do which I would want to get done. These are not all big things. I would like to clean some things off my desk. There are some things in my pockets I would like to get rid of. Then why don't I do these things? Wouldn't I be wise to get it done right now?

If I had only from now until this Sunday night to remain in this world, there would be some persons I would like to thank. I have intended to do this again and again. Then shouldn't I give myself a little tip? The thing for me to do is to go right now and get this done. There may be some people I want to forgive. I would not want to go to my grave thinking about what they have done wrong to me, or what I thought was wrong. If I want to be rid of all that, why not forgive them now? Let them go, as we say, "let them off the hook." Just be done with it. You may say, "I don't want to." That becomes your problem. In case you do not do this, you will have this hanging over you to the very last day. There are also people for whom I want to pray. I haven't prayed for them the way I really should have and I would regret it if I died before I did.

Now let me add all that up and look it right in the face. What shall I do? Pray, before the sun sets. As for the people I would like to visit, why don't I do it? Now is the time. There are people who should have some message from me; so why do I not write to them? What I am saying is that since we know the time is uncertain, and it could be short, we should remember the prayer: "So teach us to number our days, that we may apply our hearts unto wisdom." And what would be wisdom? Doing the things I have suggested. Isaiah was sent to Hezekiah, the king, to give a message: "Thus saith the Lord, Set thine house in order: for thou shalt die, and not live" (Isa. 38:1). That was really a great mercy to Hezekiah; he would have been a wise man if he had accepted God's guidance. That will not happen with everybody; but some people are given time to get ready, as it were; time to prepare to die.

Another thing I haven't mentioned which is very practical, not so much for the sake of the money that is involved, but really for the sake of other people. Each of us should make our will. If you need to see a lawyer, see one. Get down in black and white what you want done with what you leave behind.

In this way we can get ready for death: we can actually prepare for it. We could take advantage of the fact that we are now living, and we know what to do. If you are not a believer, if you are not trusting in the Lord Jesus Christ right now, you could turn to God now! What will you gain by delaying? You are running a risk. Why not turn to God now? If you are a believer and you are ready to put your trust in the Lord, why not turn everything over to Him? He is your Friend, and you can leave all in His hands. You will not need to finish anything, or explain anything. You can leave all in His hands, and you will be blessed.

5
Death
Brings
Separation

Why should death be called an enemy?

It is common to feel this way about death. This is hinted at in the familiar words in the Book of Ruth.

And Ruth said, Intreat me not to leave thee, or to return from following after thee: for whither thou goest, I will go; and where thou lodgest, I will lodge: thy people shall be my people, and thy God my God: where thou diest, will I die, and there will I be buried: the Lord do so to me, and more also, if aught but death part thee and me (Ruth 1:16-17).

These are very familiar, famous words. Here death is considered the one factor that could and does separate. In writing of the great triumph over death Paul discusses the resurrection, and has this to say, "The last enemy that shall be destroyed is death."

In what way can death be an enemy? How can it threaten anyone? How can darkness do us harm? And how can emptiness matter? We have seen that death was included in the judgment of God upon sin. "The soul that sinneth it shall die," and "the wages of sin is death." And we have seen that if we follow the way of disobedience to God we will come to naught, and to destruction. But in what sense is death an enemy now? Actually it is not so much an enemy to the person who dies, as it is for those who are bereaved. To understand how death is an enemy we need to stop and think about what is precious. What really matters so far as we are concerned? In the common sense of all men the most precious thing we have in this world is our loved ones, those with whom we have fellowship, who belong to us and to whom we belong. Anything that would harm our loved ones or impoverish our loved ones would be an enemy. This is what death will do. Consider what people do when a loved one falls deathly sick. Business, pleasure — nothing matters, men will do anything if only the loved one may live.

We have great interest and concern that we continue our fellowship with our loved ones. This is what makes Ruth's vow so sweet. She wanted fellowship with Naomi.

Real tragedy came into David's life after his sin with Bathsheba, when the prophet Nathan told him the child would die. David clung to the possibility that this might not happen and for a whole week he exercised himself in fruitless, futile prayer. He would not eat. He would not change his clothes. He did not shave himself. He devoted his whole time to calling on God. Then the child died and an amazing thing happened. When David heard the child was dead he got up and washed, shaved, put on fresh clothing, and took up his normal routine of duties. His friends came to him and said, "While the child was living you were in great distress and now that he is dead you are going about your business." Then David told them, "He will never come back. I will go to be with him." Death was final and it separated him from his child.

Later another son, Absalom, rebelled against his

father and engaged the king's army in battle. During the battle Absalom was killed. When David heard that Absalom had died he cried out, in what is considered one of the most pathetic utterances in literature, "O my son Absalom, my son, my son Absalom! would God I had died for thee, O Absalom, my son, my son!" These words show such depth of grief, even though the son was rebellious, because as father he had been separated from his son.

So death is, indeed, an enemy. Just as David was comforted in the death of his child, so is the believer comforted today. As a matter of fact for the believer separation is not the outlook. This is not the way believers feel with reference to death.

> But I would not have you to be ignorant, brethren, concerning them which are asleep, that ye sorrow not, even as others which have no hope. For if we believe that Jesus died and rose again, even so them also which sleep in Jesus will God bring with him. For this we say unto you by the word of the Lord, that we which are alive and remain unto the coming of the Lord shall not prevent them which are asleep. For the Lord himself shall descend from heaven with a shout, with the voice of the archangel, and with the trump of God: and the dead in Christ shall rise first: then we which are alive and remain shall be caught up together with them in the clouds, to meet the Lord in the air: and so shall we ever be with the Lord. Wherefore comfort one another with these words (I Thess. 4:13-18).

Is this not a wonderful passage? "Comfort one another with these words." So far as death is concerned, we cannot deny its reality. Death *is* real, but we need not fear it. We can look through it and beyond it. It is true death threatens our joy and fellowship with loved ones, but Christ Jesus has robbed death of its sting. We shall not be separated from them forever. Here is the essence of the joy of the believer. He has the promise that such separation is only temporary. Some years ago these words were written in a poem:

I cannot say, and I will not say
That he is dead! He is just away!

With a cheery smile, and a wave of the hand,
He has wandered into an unknown land,

And left us dreaming how very fair
It must be, since he lingers there.

And you — O you, who the wildest yearn
For the old-time step and the glad return —

Think of him faring on, as dear
In the love of There as the love of Here;

Mild and gentle as he was brave,
When the sweetest love of his life he gave

To simple things: where the violets grew
Pure as the eyes they were likened to,

The touches of his hands have strayed
As reverently as his lips have prayed.

Think of him still as the same, I say;
He is not dead—he is just away!"

"Away" — James Whitcomb Riley

This is what every believer should remember: we are separated from our loved ones only for a time. Christ Jesus has conquered death so death does not have the power to threaten us with everlasting separation from our loved ones.

I remember so well the occasion when one of my

sons and I were being taken by a friend to see the body of my son-in-law who had just died. In the car with us was his daughter, thirteen years of age. When we reached the funeral home she said she would not come in. Just before I got out of the car she said to me, "Poppa, that is not Daddy you will see in there. That is just the house he lived in. He has gone to be with the Lord."

Let us keep in mind that Christ Jesus has robbed the grave of its victory and has taken the sting out of death. Death is real but it is not forever. Death is unavoidable but we can pass through it. Death is no blank wall. It is a doorway and we pass through to the other side. There is one thing for sure: when we go out of this world, we go into His presence: "Absent from the body, present with the Lord." This is the great comfort of believers and this means that when our loved ones go, they are not gone forever. Just for awhile.

6
Christ Jesus Suffered Death

Do you understand why the whole idea of death is so different to a believer?

But we see Jesus, who was made a little lower than the angels for the suffering of death, crowned with glory and honour; that he by the grace of God should taste death for every man. For it became him, for whom are all things, and by whom are all things, in bringing many sons unto glory, to make the captain of their salvation perfect through sufferings. For both he that sanctifieth and they who are sanctified are all of one: for which cause he is not ashamed to call them brethren, saying, I will declare thy name unto my brethren, in the midst of the church will I sing praise unto thee. And again, I will put my trust in him. And again, Behold I and the children which God hath given me. Forasmuch then as the children are partakers of flesh and blood, he also himself likewise took part of the same; that through death he might destroy him that had the power of death, that is, the devil; and deliver them who through fear of death were all their lifetime subject to bondage. For verily he took not on him the nature of angels;

but he took on him the seed of Abraham. Wherefore in all things it behooved him to be made like unto his brethren, that he might be a merciful and faithful high priest in things pertaining to God, to make reconciliation for the sins of the people. For in that he himself hath suffered being tempted, he is able to succour them that are tempted (Heb. 2:9-18).

We are thinking about the Biblical view of death, an event that is known to all mankind. Death is feared and hated. It is something a person would like to avoid, which one dreads. It is known to all. "It is appointed unto men once to die" (Heb. 9:27); but what death means is quite different with different people. All men recognize that it is final so far as this world is concerned. Many have the feeling there is something very real about the saying, "You will be a long time dead. That is all there is."

Yet the Bible teaches new truth about death. It is a fact that for believers there is another world; we do not exit from this world into nothing. We are not even going some place where we shall have to do something to get right. We sing, "Shall we gather at the river?" but there isn't really a river to cross. Actually, when we pass out of this world we will be there immediately. There is no great distance from here to there. The Bible teaches that, and in this very fact — this new truth about death—the whole idea of death is changed. This change in the idea of death is grounded in the fact that Christ Jesus, the Son of God, came into this world for the express purpose of suffering death. It is common for us to think of Jesus of Nazareth as our example in living; we are inclined to say to one another, and especially to children, that He came into this world to show us how to live perfectly. I can accept that in a broad sense, if it is understood He showed us by living perfectly how to die.

The great fact is that when Christ Jesus died, He did not remain dead. He told His disciples that when He was put to death He would rise from the dead on the third day. This means that instead of the grave being a hole in the ground that a person is put into, it is as if the Lord Jesus (to use a rather cumbersome illustration) just knocked the other end out so far as the grave is concerned. To be sure, the grave is entered as if the body were put into a hole in the ground; but the grave is not an empty, dark place. We are passing through. The grave becomes a tunnel and we come out of it on the other side into the presence of God. This fact has drained out of death much that was sinister, harsh, and ugly. The exit is here but it becomes an entrance. Because of Christ the idea of death has been modified for the believer who can call to mind, "My Lord was here, and He faced this and went through it, too."

As we have been thinking about death, most of our ideas have been natural in origin. For instance, we began by pointing out that death comes to all. There is certainly no question about that and everybody in the world knows it. Death is the result of sin. This is based upon Scripture but our consciences also bear witness to it. We accept the idea. It is seen in Genesis that the wages of sin is death; and in Romans 5:12 Paul pointed out that as by the sin of one man death entered into the world, so all have been under death. This is a natural fact. We also took note that fear of death is bondage, and that one of the grim aspects of death is that it is unavoidable. Another sad aspect of death is that it brings separation. All of this is what death primarily means to the natural man.

But on the other hand, the Bible presents death

within a spiritual context. The natural person, when thinking about death, is distressed because it means to him the end of everything. But the Bible, in presenting to us the fact that Jesus of Nazareth suffered death and rose from the dead, presents death in a spiritual context. Death is not the end — it is the transition. The whole outlook is changed when we realize that something bright and glorious will follow death. In the natural context death is a dour subject — it is like going from daylight to darkness, from warmth to cold. But in the Scriptures, God is revealed as being there in grace and mercy.

The natural man, with no faith in God, with no promise of eternal life, has only this world in which to find blessedness and peace. The spiritual man knows that the living God is over all and makes all things work together for good. Even though death is undesirable, even though death has an aspect about it that continues to make it an enemy in a very real sense, yet the spiritual person who believes in the Lord Jesus Christ does not have to be afraid of death because of what Christ has done.

While we recognize and appreciate the natural man's fear of death, we will say that we are skeptical about any poetic imagination which talks about death as if it were something nice. There are those who seek to convey the idea that there are aspects of death that could be desirable so that one could actually be glad about it. However, such poems have all borrowed ideas from the Christian view. They seem to assume that every person will be graciously dealt with after death. But this is not true even though that is the way it *could* be. The gospel has told the world there will be life after death. Promises of comfort have been publicized all around the world. Many people readily recognize these words:

Let not your heart be troubled: ye believe in God, believe also in me. In my Father's house are many mansions: if it were not so, I would have told you. I go to prepare a place for you. And if I go and prepare a place for you, I will come again, and receive you unto myself; that where I am, there ye may be also (John 14:1-3).

These are wonderful words of life. We can appreciate the Scripture that says, "Wherefore comfort one another with these words" (I Thess. 4:18). But when poets imply that everyone will share this blessedness they are actually misleading people. We wish everybody would share it, but it is not right to let people think they can live as they like in this world, and that God will take them to bliss in the world to come. Nothing in the Bible supports such a wrong idea. Christ Jesus died to save from death — that is true. But He died to save from death all who *believe*, and those who do not believe will surely die in their sins.

Believing in the Lord Jesus Christ means more than accepting the record as true. It is true, as we have noted earlier, that death comes to all. The believer remembers that Jesus Christ will raise up whosoever believeth in Him, so that death has been robbed of that grim aspect. The apostle Paul, in writing about this, said,

But I would not have you to be ignorant, brethren, concerning them which are asleep, that ye sorrow not, even as others which have no hope. For if we believe that Jesus died and rose again, even so them also which sleep in Jesus will God bring with him (I Thess. 4:13-14).

He discusses this further, finally pointing out that when the Lord returns all of those who were already with Him and those who are here in this world waiting for Him will be taken up together to be with the Lord in the air. Then he says again, " . . . comfort one another with these words" (I Thess. 4:18).

I stress these things because I want you to understand why death has been changed for the believer. Death has lost its sting; the grave has lost its victory. When the believer dies he goes to be with Christ. The believer may look at death and see it in the natural context as the end, separation, and coming judgment, but then he will remember that the Lord Himself suffered death in order to change it. Death may be new and strange to me, but it is not new to the Lord, who passed through it. The believer facing death will not go alone. The Lord Himself will be with him. Death has often been associated with rejection; but this is not true for those in the Lord. It is true that He died, but He did not remain dead and, by His grace, neither will we.

We have sought to bring to your mind the fact that for the believer death has actually been changed. We do not see as others do. Some of us can remember instances of those we have known who have gone through death. I often think of a young woman — perhaps twenty-one years of age — who was dying. Her illness was a lingering one so that she was confined to her bed for several years. It was my custom every Sunday afternoon to spend an hour or so with her. It occurred to me that if anybody was going to talk to this girl about spiritual matters it would have to be me, being her pastor. I felt that I should speak to her and yet I felt hesitant because I did not know how to go about it. On one particular occasion when I was very quiet she said, "You are sober today. Are you worried?" I said, "Yes, I am." When she asked if I was worried about her I answered in the affirmative. She then said, "What have I done?" Then, because she had opened the door for me to speak, I said, "Dorothy, do you know that you are a very sick girl?" To that she replied, "Are you asking if I know I am going to die?" Then with a smile, "Oh, you know, there are many things worse than death." At those words my soul just sang. Oh, how I wished that I could share that truth with everybody in the world, that they might realize there are things really worse than death.

Of course I realize there cannot be anything much worse than death for the natural person, for one who has no prospect for the future; but Dorothy Roberts did have. She expected to meet the Lord. When I preached her funeral sermon two days later, the text I took was, "If ye loved me, ye would rejoice, because I said, I go unto the Father" (John 14:28). Dorothy showed me that the prospect of leaving this world and going into the presence of God held no terror at all. It warms my heart to think that those who believe in the Lord can look death in the face with such composure. He is able to give them the confidence and the assurance that enables them to look beyond it into the glory of His presence.

This is the significance of robbing death of its sting. Paul says "the sting of death is sin," and we have pointed out that Christ carried away our sins. So actually the experience of death is just something that happens en route. When we have a spiritual frame of mind we are conscious of eternal things. We know that even while we are here we are in His presence, and when we will be there, we will yet be in His presence, so that our going on through death into the presence of our God is all in His perfect plan for us.

I suspect there are some who, when they think about that, will say, "But I haven't been what I ought to have been." I can assure you He will be there to cover you with Himself. Some may have the feeling, "When I come into the presence of God, that is when I will be judged and dealt with according to what I have done." Let me remind you that if you are a believer in the Lord Jesus Christ, you went into the presence of God and settled your case out of court. You confessed that you were guilty, that you had done wrong, and you claimed His promise to be gracious. He forgave you and that forgiveness has never been rescinded. The fact that Christ Jesus came here has opened the way for you to follow Him with assurance. Even though you remember sins that you may not even like to think about, you can remember that He took care of all that, too.

If a believer is thinking, "When the time comes for me to die I will be scared, uneasy," let him turn his heart and mind to the Lord, and ask Him for grace. He can give it to him, and he can find quietness and peace. He died for the believer, let him believe it. His blood will cleanse him from all sin: let him believe it.

There may be some who will feel that in death everything is over — everything in this world. Yes, that's right. But when I leave this world I will not leave much. I will have something far, far better; because going out of this world into the presence of God is like going out of something that is clay into something that is gold: out of darkness into the light. It was a marvelous thing that Christ Jesus suffered death and was raised from the dead. Because of that, you and I can follow Him as we enter into death, and we can expect to be raised from the dead with Him.

7
Death
Is
Defeated

Do you understand why a believer need not fear death?

The Biblical view of death is entirely different from the natural man's view. The common, popular view of death such as you and I encounter in talking to people is the natural one, and if I should have that point of view it is, as it were, from where I stand until I draw the last breath. That would be what death means to me — from here I move up to the end. But that is not the Biblical view. It is true that every human being lives in the shadow of death. Not only do we hear about it every day, and we see it around us continually, but our own day is coming and we know it. Each day is one day nearer that last moment when death takes over. There is no reason for us to turn our backs, hide our faces, and bury our heads in the sands like an ostrich. It may not be pleasant but it is real. It may not be the kind of thinking to make us happy but it is honest.

As human beings when we think of death, naturally we shrink. Even when we call upon our inward strength and show a sort of stoic resolution to see it through, when it comes we are nonetheless fearful. We know that we can die and we know that we must die. Sometimes, by way of emphasizing that, I am inclined to point out that dying is one thing we can do when we can't do anything else. But we shudder at the prospect — until we look up to God. It is time now for us to keep this in mind. We are thinking of the Biblical view of death, and when the Bible looks at death, God is in the picture: we bring Him to mind. Here is one aspect of the glorious victory that each believer in Christ Jesus has in the Lord Himself.

Death will come. Yes, I know, and to me, also. But my Lord has opened a way through death. It is for me to look for and see that way to life. Every threat of death has been nullified; every fear of death that lingers in my heart is groundless. We remember the gracious words of the Lord Jesus Christ:

> Let not your heart be troubled: ye believe in God, believe also in me. In my Father's house are many mansions: if it were not so, I would have told you. I go to prepare a place for you. And if I go and prepare a place for you, I will come again, and receive you unto myself; that where I am, there ye may be also (John 14:1-3).

Wonderful, precious words — spoken all over the world in more than fifteen hundred languages and dialects. Christ Jesus came into the picture and He has changed it so that I need not let my heart be troubled.

Actually, death is my just fate because of my sins. I realize that it came because of the sin of Adam, but I need not hide behind that. My own conscience is very clear about this: I have sinned and come short of the glory of God. I recognize the fact that as a sinner I have forfeited my right to receive the blessings of God. But my Lord Jesus Christ, the Son of God, carried away my sin. I will tell the whole wide world that I have been set free. I am free from guilt. I know I have done wrong, but the blood of the Lord Jesus Christ is able to cleanse me from all sin. When I believe that, the sting of death is gone. Death is defeated. It does not have any punch. Death will be necessary and I am going through it, but it cannot separate me from the Lord. He has freed me from guilt.

Someone might say, "It is just not fair." That may be right. No doubt it isn't fair, and I am thankful to God it isn't. If I were to get my just deserts I would never be able to look forward to heaven. But you see, I am going to receive the grace of God; the kindness and love of God which He has shown toward even those who are not His. He said, "In a day when they sought me not, I found them." It will be like that.

In the third place, death looms ominously as a dark cloud over my whole soul, seeming to herald a storm in my future, but do you know what I can think about? "The Lord is my refuge and strength." I know that death is like a dark cloud, but when I think about death I think about the Lord being my refuge and strength. I want to keep in my mind and heart that Almighty God has given His Son, the Lord Jesus Christ, to deliver me from the pangs of death.

Then in the fourth place while it is true that death is inevitable, and it is bound to come, I need not fear. The resurrection is real, and while death may be inevitable, it is not permanent. It is a transition I will pass through. How do I know I will pass through it? Because my Lord did, and I am with Him. I shall not be passing through in my own strength. The Lord Jesus Christ opened the way and He will see me through.

So we come to the fifth idea: Death threatens to separate me from my loved ones. That would be sad, but death cannot do it. You see, my loved ones are not wiped out, nor will I be wiped out. The point is, we will pass through this and we will all be together in the Lord. All believing people will be together in the Lord.

When we think about death, instead of considering it as merely an exit from here, actually death has become an entrance into there. It is not true only that I move up to death for the end of everything here, but when I move up to death it is the beginning of all that is there. Now, what is here is temporary, but what is there is eternal. What is here is many times spotted, uncertain, unsafe, and many times unclean. What is there is sure and safe and glorious. When I pass through death, which lets me out of this world, that is the very experience that lets me into the world to come, so that although once I considered death as an exit and thought of it as being the end of everything, I know now that it is the entrance and it is the beginning of all that is good and permanent, and I thank the Lord.

8
Christ Jesus Arose Triumphant

Do you know why believers rejoice in victory at Easter time?

"But God raised him from the dead." In these simple words the apostle Paul made a statement that is basic to the whole Christian gospel and refers to what is probably the greatest event that ever occurred on earth. I am speaking of Calvary and the open grave. I realize that all of the works of God in Christ are wonderful, but the one outstanding work of God that is lifted up above all others and made absolutely above and beyond and over everything is the resurrection of Jesus Christ from the dead. We all know how at Easter the church bells ring with a triumphant tone. Believers unite in singing His praises. "Up from the grave He arose with a mighty triumph o'er His foes."

There is a sweetness and a gentleness in the Christmas story of the Babe of Bethlehem, and we love it; but there is victory, there is triumph, there is the power of Almighty God in the song of the angels when they announce, "He is not here. He is risen." The resurrection of Jesus Christ is recognized as the greatest fact in history. As a matter of fact, it is the one significant happening that will cause us to change our mind about all that is in the world. There have been miracles performed by Almighty God through the Lord Jesus Christ and through His prophets that are really wonderful and all of them are significant, but the resurrection of the body of Jesus of Nazareth after He had lain in the grave for three days must remain the most amazing and wonderful thing that has ever occurred on the face of the earth.

After Jesus had cleansed the temple He was asked, "What sign shewest thou unto us, seeing that thou doest these things" (John 2:18)? He answered plainly, "There shall no sign be given to it ["an evil and adulterous generation"], but the sign of the prophet Jonas: for as Jonas was three days and three nights in the whale's belly; so shall the Son of man be three days and three nights in the heart of the earth" (Matt. 12:39-40). Paul afterwards taught that if you will confess with your mouth Jesus as Lord and believe in your heart that God raised Him from the dead, you shall be saved. This means that the one thing that is necessary is to believe. You need to openly testify with your mouth that you personally recognize Jesus Christ as Lord and deep down in your heart, in your innermost being, you must be convinced absolutely, believe and commit yourself to the idea, that God raised Jesus Christ from the dead.

Do I need to point out that not everybody is going to be raised from the dead in that way? Do I need to point out that you will not be raised from the dead in Christ Jesus because you are a human being? The Bible does not say that all the trees that die will remain dead, that dogs that die will remain dead, and that horses that die will remain dead, but that because you are a man, when you die you will live again. It does not follow that way. What actually follows is this: God's own Son, Jesus of Nazareth, came into this world made in human form, with the same kind of body that we have, touched with all the feelings of our infirmities, "in everything made like as we are yet without sin." That body was done to death and put in the grave, where it remained for three days; then God raised that body from the dead. God kept Him alive and He appeared from time to time over the space of forty days and then, in full view of all, He ascended into heaven and was taken away from their sight. This is the story. This is a fact. It is tremendous; it is amazing; and it is also very important — because this followed death. Logically there could never have been a resurrection if death had not occurred. You never could have the new life that is in Christ Jesus unless you died to the old life that is in the flesh.

When we wonder in what sense Jesus' resurrection was triumphant, consider what death would have done, and how death would have dealt with Him. When His human body was here on earth and was facing death, it would be assumed that death would be final. That would be the last of it. We have already pointed out that after death there isn't any more of this world. But with the resurrection of Jesus Christ you will have to say that death is not final. There is something else afterward. A man may die and his body be buried, but God can raise him from the dead. That is the affirmation that has to be stated over and over again all over the world, and engraved on the hearts and minds of people. Death is not final because Jesus Christ rose from the dead. He ascended into heaven and is there now in the presence of God.

One of the things about death that causes us to shrink from it and feel as we do, is the separation from our loved ones. In that sense death is an enemy. But with the resurrection of Jesus Christ we rejoice in the wonderful truth that the separation will not be permanent. As Christ Jesus arose triumphant, so shall those who fall asleep in Jesus be raised up to be with Him. We which are alive and remain will be caught up together with them in the clouds, and so shall we ever be with the Lord. Do not misunderstand me. This is not because we are human beings. What I am saying is not true for every human person. What I am saying is true for "whosoever believeth in him." It is not difficult to become one of His. All you need to do is to yield yourself to the Lord and trust in Him. You must believe in Him. You must not only believe that He is the Son of God and that He died for *sinners*, but you must believe He died for *you*. He is your Savior and you are to understand this is God's way of providing for you an open entrance into His presence; you must take it to heart and receive it as true, and you will rejoice in it. When He was raised from the dead your highest hopes were confirmed. Just as surely as he was raised from the dead you will be raised from the dead, and your loved ones who have fallen asleep in Him will likewise be raised from the dead. Paul says, "So shall we ever be with the Lord," then he goes on to say, "Comfort one another with these words."

The death of the natural body ends life in this world and opens the door for judgment. "It is appointed unto men once to die, but after this the judgment" (Heb. 9:27). At this point we can see the marvelous truth in the work of Jesus Christ. Not only did He arrange that death would not be final because we are going to live again; and not only did Jesus Christ arrange that we would not be separated from our loved ones, because we will all be together with the Lord; but Almighty God, through the Lord Jesus Christ, has arranged that as far as we are concerned, we who believe in Him and have our trust in the Lord Jesus Christ will not face judgment. Judgment will not follow for the believer. Christ Jesus said, "I am come that they might have life, and that they might have it more abundantly." In Christ Jesus death is overcome. He is alive now and will be alive forever and those who trust in Him will pass through death once and they will not pass through it the second time. This is the wonderful truth that we have in the story of the resurrection of Jesus Christ. We say, "Christ Jesus arose triumphant" because that is exactly what He did, and we rejoice in it.

9
Christ Jesus Lives Forever

Do you understand why the fact that Jesus Christ is alive changes the whole idea of death?

It is common knowledge that Jesus of Nazareth lived in this world as a man. He did all the things men do and was touched with all the feelings of our infirmities. The Gospels reveal that He was no stronger physically than other men. He became weary, He knew sorrow, and He eventually died. When He was put on the cross He died just as any other man would die, although probably a little differently. He was buried the way they buried others. It is true they took special care of Him and put Him in a new grave where never a man had been laid, but still He was taken from the cross, wrapped in grave clothes, carried into the cave, and laid-down just as any other man would have been. But then something happened. He arose from the dead.

In the natural world that does not happen. Death was supposed to close the door for Him, too, but that did not happen here. The resurrection of Jesus Christ enables us to realize that the person who lives here can also live there; there is another world. Not only is this actual; it is factual and it is real. Jesus of Nazareth arose from the dead, and is alive now. He is now in a different world and is much better off, but He is the same person. That is the promise of Almighty God as to what is going to happen to believers. Since this is true that Jesus of Nazareth arose from the dead, that He became alive again, then there is another real world and this makes death different. It is not merely the painting of a doorway on a wall to sort of symbolize there could be a door there; behind that painting is the wall and behind that is nothing. Death is an actual doorway in that wall into the other world. Since Christ Jesus arose from the dead to live forever, death becomes for the believer an event that ushers him into something. He is being ushered into fellowship and communion with God, face to face with our Lord Jesus Christ

We are thinking of the resurrection of the believers, but the Bible promises the resurrection of all men, the just and the unjust. But this will be another resurrection — a different one. All men will be called into existence again to come face to face with God because right now in the presence of God, in the spiritual world, Jesus of Nazareth, the Christ of God, is alive. We do not have any revelation as to what sort of body unbelievers will have in their resurrection.

Do you know one reason why all this sounds so strange? It is because in public we talk so little about it. You see, the way we ordinarily talk about death in public is the way you and I tend to think about death. Normally we think about death the way people talk about it. That is the dark end, a passing into the unknown, and so on. But that is not the Biblical view of death. And it is not truly the believer's view of death. All that is true, humanly speaking, but more than that is true, and Jesus of Nazareth demonstrated that fact. They put Him to death. They thrust a spear into His side to make sure He was dead. Three days later He was alive and will never die again. God the Father is always alive. He was alive while Jesus was in this world, He was alive when Jesus was in the grave and when Jesus arose from the dead; in fact, He raised Jesus from the dead. The Holy Spirit is alive and He lives in the believer. Almighty God is eternal. He is everlasting. When we put our hands in His, He will take us right along with Him; death shall no more have dominion over us. That is what the Bible says.

In the communion that the believer has in fellowship with God the Father, God the Son, and God the Holy Spirit, the believer will share in "the joy of the Lord." That is a phrase that has much more in it than we ordinarily realize. Usually when we speak of the "joy of the Lord" we are inclined to think of the joy of a human being who has faith in God. When a human being truly believes in God and in the salvation of Jesus Christ, He believes in the forgiveness of sins and the reconciliation with God and the indwelling of the Holy Spirit, and he will have joy because all this is an amazing and remarkable thing. But that is not the essence of that phrase "the joy of the Lord." The joy of the Lord is the joy that the Lord has (and, by the way, that does not mean that He is dependent upon what He sees in me to be joyful). The joy of the Father would be in looking on the face of the Son and in the fellowship of the Holy Spirit. And that is a joy you and I can share. The Lord Jesus said in John 15:11, "These things have I spoken unto you, that my joy might remain in you, and that your joy might be full."

So in that communion, when the believer leaves this world and comes into the presence of God, he shares in the joy of the Lord. It is a blessed experience that he can look forward to, far more than anything he would ordinarily even know about. And there is something else true. "Wherefore he is able also to save them to the uttermost that come unto God by him, seeing he ever liveth to make intercession for them" (Heb. 7:25). The great truth in that is that the resurrection of Christ Jesus was not merely a matter of the wonderful power of God in raising a dead body in order that salvation should be made available to us who hear and obey, but the resurrection of Jesus Christ results in this: He will live always as our High Priest in the presence of God and this assures for us an effectual intercession by the Lord. He is constantly praying for us. I think believers have heard this often enough, for it lingers in the memory and encourages them to some extent to have confidence in Him; but I cannot help but feel from my fellowship with believing people wherever I have been that as a whole they have far too faint a view of this. Their awareness of this intercession is very limited. There is a wonderful song about it, "I have a Savior who's pleading in glory, and oh, that my Savior were your Savior, too." Let's not just sing about this blessing, let's live every minute in the realization of it.

Paul speaks of the high priestly ministry of intercession going on constantly, and that is apparently the saving power of the gospel (Rom. 5:10). We can count on His being alive and present in heaven, and this is a real challenge to our faith. We are to believe in Him, but what I want to emphasize here is that because this is so, death is not nearly so forbidding in its appearance. When we leave here, we are going there. "Absent from the body; present with the Lord."

10
Fellowship in Heaven Is Unbroken

Do you understand why it is that people generally feel that if they can get into heaven, worries and fears of rejection will be gone?

Death is a grim subject for men naturally, but not so for a believer. It is at the first thought that death looms harsh, but the more the believer thinks about it, the brighter the future becomes. Only for those who are uncertain about themselves and God — only for the lost soul — is death a heavy subject. To be sure, in this world there is a tragic air about death anytime. It is always shocking to us. But the believer is called upon to lift up his head and look; "there is a happy land far, far away; where saints in glory stand." He sings about it. Paul wrote to the Thessalonian Christians about this:

But I would not have you to be ignorant, brethren, concerning them which are asleep, that ye sorrow not, even as others which have no hope. For if we believe that Jesus died and rose again, even so them also which sleep in Jesus will God bring with him. For this we say unto you by the word of the Lord, that we which are alive and remain unto the coming of the Lord shall not prevent them which are asleep. For the Lord himself shall descend from heaven with a shout, with the voice of the archangel, and with the trump of God: and the dead in Christ shall rise first: then we which are alive and remain shall be caught up together with them in the clouds, to meet the Lord in the air: and so shall we ever be with the Lord. Wherefore comfort one another with these words (I Thess. 4:13-18).

Paul wrote this that we should be comforted thereby. Death is hard to face for any human being, but you and I who believe in the Lord Jesus do not have to face it alone. There is a profound difference in the outlook upon death of the natural man and of a believer. The natural man is conscious of the fact that death interrupts, death breaks off, causes separation, and involves much uncertainty. Then there is that undertone of grim significance: the final judgment at the hands of an offended God. That is the natural man's point of view and we can't blame him for turning away from it. He does not want to think about it. It will come, but he thinks, "It will be bad enough when it comes. I do not want to think about it ahead of time."

Now the believer is conscious of the providence of God that watches over all his affairs, including the last one. He can trust God. We do not know how we are going to feel when the time comes, and we do not know what we are going to do. I suppose one of the things that bothers many of us will be the thought of unfinished business. About this we can trust the providence of God. When the believer does this he feels better about it. He is conscious also of the grace of God. God is not only in control, He is not only Almighty God and sovereign, but He is gracious. He is kind. He is good. The grace of God can be expected, and while the believer may not know what he is going to go through, God does know and God will provide what he needs. The believer is also conscious of the mercy of God in which he can take refuge. The believer will have some knowledge of the glorious promises of God. The believer has heard those gracious words over and over again, "Let not your heart be troubled: ye believe in God, believe also in me. In my Father's house are many mansions: if it were not so, I would have told you" (John 14:1-2). Oh, how many times I have gone back and rested on those words. There is much about the future I don't know. But the Lord Jesus knows; Almighty God knows; and if there had been any reason at all to question the outcome in the future, He would have said so.

We realize that not much is known about heaven but no one has ever questioned the fact that it is permanent. Whatever goes on there is forever. We think a great deal about the uncertainties of this world and we wonder whether we will make this or finish that and so on, but when it comes to being in heaven, there is no further concern because that is for sure. "So shall we ever be with the Lord." We have a feeling of belonging to Him and we are trusting in Him, and He is going to take care of us. Just as fellowship with loved ones is a precious treasure, so to have it unbroken and uninterrupted is an added blessing. When we are with our loved ones, we are blessed. The longer we are with them, the more blessed we are. Now, if that blessing is unbroken — and we know for sure it will continue that way — there is no chance that it will be broken in the future and that is an added blessing.

I suspect that so far as living in this world is concerned, "Good-bye" is always one of the heaviest words.

It is hard to say, but do you know, so far as the believer is concerned, there is really no "Good-bye"? We have a saying, "So long," and what we mean is that it will be just "so long" until we see one another again. There are other ways of putting it — we have various ways of trying to get away from saying "Good-bye."

So far as the believer is concerned there will be no separation there. Remember this particularly when you think of death. The believer may be uneasy about the actual experience. I don't know how it will strike you. It may strike you that the actual experience of death may possibly involve pain or some kind of calamity. It may involve some distress, but it may not. I have just heard about a good friend, a great man, who passed away in his sleep. That can happen. Or it can be that death can be seen coming, and then it is frightening. But it can come to us even when we are not looking for it. There is no assurance about the time; but one thing we can know for sure — no matter how we feel about it and no matter how uncertain or uneasy we may be, we know the Lord leads here, too, and we put our trust in Him.

One thing I want to stress is the fellowship that we will have in heaven with the Lord and with our own loved ones — "so shall we ever be with the Lord." As previously noted, there will be no separation there; this takes away much of the sting of death. Believers are not able to face death with composure because they are so strong; believers do not face death with a sense of assurance because they are so good; and believers do not face death with a sense of confidence because they know so much. It is because they are in Christ Jesus. He is good. He is strong. He knows everything and He has given us His Word. When we are thinking about death and are getting the Biblical view of death, we need to remember this is not death for everybody. Certainly all men will die, but some men are believers, and some men are not believers. When unbelievers die, it is a different matter. Those who are not believers have nothing to look forward to that gives them any hope. All they have is an adding up, a settling of their accounts as they are when they die in their sins. It is no wonder they dread it. They should! But so far as the believer is concerned, his sins are forgiven. They are taken away and now, when he looks forward, he has a bright day coming by and by. He is coming into the very presence of the living God who is merciful and gracious.

11
Glory
Is
Coming

Do believers have any real reason for not dreading death?

Believers tell each other and the whole wide world that death is swallowed up in victory. There is no point in seeking to deny the reality of death. Poets and philosophers may seek to talk it away. Poets will make imaginary and fanciful talk, and if one listens to them the impression may come that everything will be as sweet and rosy as that particular poet describes it to be. The philosopher will explain until he has explained away the very fact that you know — that men die. And when men die, all the abrupt, awful, frightful, and dreadful aspects of death crowd in on the heart and mind. Despite what the poets and philosophers may have tried to do by talking about it, the Grim Reaper goes on his way, undisturbed.

All men die. The wicked die. The godly die. "It is appointed unto man once to die." Believers do claim that death has lost its sting, and this is what I now want to comment about. The more I have thought about this I have been increasingly impressed with the fact that when we keep looking at death from the point of view of a believer, it shrinks. It is not nearly so frightful, or so dark and horrible. It gets pale and dim and light. It should be remembered that in everything we are saying about the Biblical view of death we must keep in mind that the Bible is written for people who believe. The world calls them Christians — people who believe in Jesus Christ. Every claim we make about death is made on behalf of those who believe in Christ. For those who believe in Christ, death is still real and death is always an enemy. It interrupts what is going on. Death always ends happy things that are going on. It breaks up fellowship and separates loved ones. For those reasons we can't like it. It will break up homes and for that reason we dread it; it will stop works that are going on that are helping people, and that causes us to wonder time and time again. Death is ugly and grim, but those who believe in the Lord Jesus Christ rejoice in the victory that was won by Him.

The eternal Son of God became flesh. He took upon Himself the nature of Adam for the suffering of death. Jesus of Nazareth was put to death in this world, buried in this world, but on the third day in this world "up from the grave He arose, with a mighty triumph o'er His foes." That changes the picture. Christ Jesus is alive now and Christ Jesus is coming again. This is why He could promise His disciples:

> Let not your heart be troubled: ye believe in God, believe also in me. In my Father's house are many mansions: if it were not so, I would have told you. I go to prepare a place for you. And if I go and prepare a place for you, I will come again, and receive you unto myself; that where I am, there ye may be also (John 14:1-3).

Every single word in those verses needs to be etched in gold. It is all there — true. That is the end of the dread. It can be the end of the fear of anybody — "whosoever believeth in him." The angels will come and stand by him and will say a word into his heart, "This same Jesus . . . shall so come in like manner as ye have seen him go into heaven" (Acts 1:11). When Christ Jesus came into this world, He came as a babe and He was laid in a manger — humble, helpless, harmless — the Lamb of God. But when He comes again, He will come as a conquering victor, the Lion of the Tribe of Judah, demonstrating His superiority and His triumph over every enemy, including death.

All the world dreads the day of judgment because there is no man who sinneth not. Some people are wicked, some are godly. Some who are wicked want to be like that, while some are indifferent about it. But they stay that way. There are people who are turned to God and they want to seek God's face. Seldom do they feel they are as close as they could be. Seldom are they able to do what they want to do, but they look up to Him and they trust Him. It is true there is no man who sinneth not. But there is a difference between those who die in their sins, and those who have faced God and confessed their sins. Those who die in their sins will face the judgment of God. It is true for them that it is appointed unto man once to die and after that the judgment, and in connection with that, the Scripture says this stern word, "It is a fearful thing to fall into the hands of the living God."

The natural man shrinks at the idea of death, trembles even, and does not want to think about death. I don't blame him. He has every right to act that way because it is not going to be easy for him. He is going right into the presence of God to give an account of everything he has ever done, every idle word he has spoken and when he meets our God he is going to find out that our God is a consuming fire. I know that sounds hard and almost threatening, but it is very, very true. The marvelous thing is that a man does not *need* to face it that way. Those who turn to God in repentance and in faith are forgiven. Listen to this word of Scripture, "There is therefore now no condemnation to them which are in Christ Jesus" (Rom. 8:1). Can you lay hold of this idea? It is possible for you, no matter who you are, "though your sins be as scarlet, they shall be as white as snow; though they be red like crimson, they shall be as wool" (Isa. 1:18). Do you realize that? This is for you. All you need to do is turn to and cling to Him. The believer can look forward and upward with confidence and joy. Death is real. Christ is real. Heaven is real. Death is not the end of everything. It is a phase, an event in the course of living. It is the end of this life and it is the beginning of the next. It is an exit so far as this world is concerned, and an entrance so far as that world is concerned. When believers die, it is not all over, they then go into the presence of God.

When Jesus of Nazareth was just a few days old His parents took Him into the temple for the ceremony of circumcision. As they brought Him in, Simeon, an old, godly man who had served at the temple for years and years, lifted up his voice when he saw Jesus of Nazareth, the Babe of Bethlehem, and said, "Lord, now lettest thou thy servant depart in peace, according to thy word: for mine eyes have seen thy salvation, which thou hast prepared before the face of all people; a light to lighten the Gentiles, and the glory of thy people Israel" (Luke 2:29-32). He was talking about Jesus and he was able to say to Almighty God, "Now I can go home. Now I can die. I have had what you promised me. You promised me I wouldn't die until I saw His face and now I have seen it." This was the way he felt.

If we are believers in the Lord Jesus Christ we can walk right up and look death in the face and know this: as ugly as it is and as frightening as it is, just in itself, beyond it lies the Glory Land and

> When all my labors and trials are o'er
> And I am safe on that beautiful shore,
> Just to be near the dear Lord I adore,
> Will through the ages be glory for me.

The great Glory Song emphasizes this expectation of the believer. I tell you, it is wonderful. We have a glorious, golden future. God is going to magnify the name of the Lord Jesus Christ before our eyes and give us a great joy in Him and we thank Him.

12
In
Mighty
Triumph

Do you know which event in the career of Jesus Christ showed His almighty power in the clearest fashion?

Jesus of Nazareth performed many works of wonder and power, but the outstanding miracle above all others was His resurrection. He arose from the dead. The gospel tells the world that God sent His Son into the world to seek and to save the lost. To "save" means "to deliver from danger, to deliver from calamity, to deliver from loss."

Man's life is perhaps his most precious possession and the one event most feared and dreaded is death. Some have wondered about the situation in this world. Every living thing must die. This may account for the sadness that haunts so many. Life is limited. "The grass withereth, the flower fadeth" (Isa. 40:8). We are conscious of this. The natural outlook is depressing. Paul refers to this when he writes to the Romans:

For I reckon that the sufferings of this present time are not worthy to be compared with the glory which shall be revealed in us. For the earnest expectation of the creature waiteth for the manifestation of the sons of God. For the creature was made subject to vanity, not willingly, but by reason of him who hath subjected the same in hope, because the creature itself also shall be delivered from the bondage of corruption into the glorious liberty of the children of God. For we know that the whole creation groaneth and travaileth in pain together until now (Rom. 8:18-22).

Paul is saying something very obvious to everyone, but there is a golden thread of hope in the gospel. Jesus Christ was the Lamb slain before the foundation of the world. Apparently before anything was created the Son of God had already committed Himself to do what was necessary to deliver this mortal creation from the bondage of death. And this deliverance from death is made available to all who believe in Him. We need only put our trust in Him. He does the work and has the power to accomplish this deed. He will save forever those who come to Him. God gave Him the power to raise from the dead anyone whom He would.

But the Scriptures reveal that this is not only the promise of Almighty God in Christ; Christ actually performed this work. It would have been true and valid if He had only given His word, but God actually demonstrated His will in the resurrection of the body of Jesus Christ. Yet the resurrection reveals more than His grace and His glory.

The career of Jesus Christ did not end with His being raised from the dead. That is not the last word in the story; He showed Himself to be alive for forty days. I have often thought about that. We say it so quickly and so easily. But what a tremendous experience for the disciples when the living Lord Jesus Christ showed Himself alive from time to time for more than a month!

Then, at the end of the forty days, He ascended into heaven in full view of His disciples. They stood watching Him go and heard those angels say to them, "Ye men of Galilee, why stand ye gazing up into heaven? this same Jesus, which is taken up from you into heaven, shall so come in like manner as ye have seen him go into heaven" (Act 1:11).

We notice, then, that when the Lord Jesus Christ left here His work was not finished. He is now at the right hand of God (Stephen saw Him there) and He is praying for us. In my own case, and I am afraid that for many other Christians as well, it is all too true that we forget this so easily; think of it so seldom. He is praying for us right now. He is Almighty. You may say, "Well, that would be all right if I were good." That is not the point. It would be all right if you trusted Him. "There is none righteous, no, not one" (Rom. 3:10). The Lord knows this and He is praying for us, and He will come again with great glory. Because of all this, death has lost its terror for the believer. After all, we are not coming up to a blank wall. It is a doorway. We will pass through into the light. This world is a dark place; that world has no night, so death has lost its terror. In speaking of the promised Messiah, Isaiah said: "He will swallow up death in victory; and the Lord God will wipe away tears from off all faces; and the rebuke of his people shall he take away from off all the earth: for the Lord hath spoken it" (Isa. 25:8).

That is exactly what God will do. When you and I think about death, the Biblical or Christian view of death, we can know that the believer no longer need fear death because it is not the end of his living. It is the end of this world but he is passing on through the doorway into the world to come.

Because of sin, souls have been spoken of as being

in the prisonhouse of death. Human beings are in bondage because of the fear that death is inevitable and final. No one with enough understanding to know his right hand from his left is not concerned about the fact that one of these days — and he doesn't know which one — will be his last. For the believer, however, all of this is changed. Christ Jesus died for our sins, was buried, and was raised on the third day. Christ Jesus burst the bands of death. By carrying away our sins He has set us forever free from guilt and free from sin.

When He returns, He will bring with Him those who have fallen asleep in Jesus, and so shall we ever be with the Lord. That is the prospect, and for the believer this looking forward to passing on into the presence of God can become a quiet, joyful anticipation. I hope that you may have had an experience where you have actually seen it happen among your family or among your friends, where people have died with composure and even with joy. You could almost see what was happening. Many people bear witness and testimony, "I don't know why it was, but just at the last, just before she went away, her face was beautiful." Others have said, "I don't know what he was thinking about, but I know that just at the last, before he breathed his last, it was as though he saw something wonderful." A great many believing people pass out of this world into the presence of God with joy, with expectation. It is not so much that they wanted to leave their family and friends, or that they wanted release. It is that they were looking into His face, and they beheld the Lamb of God who gave Himself for them.

I remember one of my boyhood friends. He became a believer and whenever we could we had fellowship together. Whenever we met we spent all of our time talking about the Lord. He "went home," as we say, from a heart condition. His brother was taking him to his doctor. As they started toward the car he said, "Don't bother taking me. The Lord has told me He is coming for me shortly and this is all a waste of time. In no time at all He will be here." As they started through the door my friend slumped to the floor. He was gone. He knew he was going and he went with composure, with quietness and peace. There have been many other such incidents.

Such quiet composure does not come from personal will power. We do not get this because we have strong inner fortitude. Actually, when a person dies the ground is cut out from under him. There is nothing left and if he is going to be able to face death with peace in his heart, he will need to have help. The glorious truth is that it is available. Almighty God has sent His Son for that very purpose. Christ Jesus did not come into this world to stop death, but to go through it. We are told He died for all men; anybody can be saved: " . . . whosoever believeth in him should not perish but have everlasting life." That is all there is to it — whosoever will, may; and whosoever won't will not. That is fair. Calvary was not the end. Christ Jesus arose from the dead and He was given power to raise from the dead whomsoever He would. So we are urged to look to Jesus, the author and finisher of our faith, even in the very hour of death.

As we think about death we remember that when we die we will come face to face with God. When we think about coming face to face with God it is natural that we think about our sins. We then will have a sense of fear, because we are impressed by the idea of going into the presence of Almighty God, who knows us like an open book. It is proper to feel fear. But when we speak of "our sins" to the believer, we need to remember that Christ Jesus carried them away. We are reconciled to God, so that every thought about our sins can actually be the basis for a moment of joy. He carried away every single thing that was wrong.

Also when we come face to face with God we may be conscious of our weakness. We think, "Well, I am just not much. I don't have any strength." That condition of heart and mind is actually a broken and contrite heart, which the Lord will not despise. When we come face to face with God we do not have to be afraid. We do not have to look on Him as if He were some judge, ready to condemn. All of that is in the past since we believe in Him. We have confessed our sins and "he is faithful and just to forgive us our sins and to cleanse us from all unrighteousness." The sting of death is sin and the strength of sin is the law. If the idea should come to my mind that "I am going to get what I deserve," then I need to believe His promises and rejoice because I can say at once: "Not when I am a believer." This is what Christ Jesus died for, and when we come face to face with God we will lift up our heart and lift up our eyes and look into His face: He is ready to receive us: He is our Father. He will take us to Himself — not because we earned it; not because we worked for it, not because we are good. Oh, no! It is because the Lord Jesus Christ is gracious and merciful; He gave Himself for us, and He will bring us into the presence of God.

A person might ask: "What shall I do?" Such a person should thank Him and praise Him. He should lift up his heart and rejoice. When we think about death we know that we are coming to the end of living in the flesh. So far as life in this world is concerned, that will be finished; but we do not stop there. He didn't. He ended His life here and was put in the grave, but He arose from the dead! And He will raise all who believe in Him. Our hope is in Him and He lives forever. He gives eternal life. A person might say, "I am not thinking about eternal life in heaven. I am thinking about living here on earth just now." Let such a soul look into His face. He has it set up for "whosoever believeth" to take that person to Himself and He will be with that believer all the way.

Perhaps there may be someone who, in spite of all these promises, still feels dismay at the thought of death — one who may still be scared. To such a soul I would emphasize that you will not have to face it alone. Remember, "Let not your heart be troubled: ye believe in God, believe also in me. In my Father's house are many mansions: if it were not so, I would have told you. I go to prepare a place for you. And if I go and prepare a place for you, I will come again, and receive you unto myself; that where I am, there ye may be also" (John 14:1-3). Keep that in mind. If you are a believer you will not come to the edge of death without the Lord Jesus Christ meeting you with outstretched hands and arms. He will take you to Himself.

When we think about death we have in mind that we are going into the unknown, but here I want to remind you that He said, "I will not leave you comfortless." By these words He is saying, "I am not going to leave you to be orphans." Looking into His face, fears vanish. Doubts dissolve. Uncertainty is gone. Death is real but we are no longer afraid. You will remember those passages that we have many, many times quoted from Scripture. In Isaiah 25:8-9 we read:

He will swallow up death in victory; and the Lord God will wipe away tears from off all faces; and the rebuke of his people shall he take away from off all the earth: for the Lord hath spoken it. And it shall be said in that day, Lo, this is our God; we have waited for him, and he will save us: this is the Lord; we have waited for him, we will be glad and rejoice in his salvation.

In Revelation 21:3-4 we read:

Behold, the tabernacle of God is with men, and he will dwell with them, and they shall be his people, and God himself shall be with them, and be their God. And God shall wipe away all tears from their eyes; and there shall be no more death, neither sorrow, nor crying, neither shall there be any more pain: for the former things are passed away.

At the time a friend of our family passed away my wife was moved to put some of her thoughts into a poem that has been a blessing to many. Here is the poem:

Call it not death
When swift release from suffering and pain
Heralds a Kingdom free from ills:
A glorious reign.

Call it not death
When visions fair dispel this earthly night
And those things now but darkly seen
Become as light.

Call it not death
When heavenly hosts in radiant array
Welcome the liberated soul
To endless day.

—Sarah Bernstein Gutzke

Here is a hymn that for many years I have called
one of my favorites:

Abide with me: fast falls the eventide;
The darkness deepens; Lord, with me abide:
When other helpers fail, and comforts flee,
Help of the helpless, O abide with me!

Swift to its close ebbs out life's little day;
Earth's joys grow dim, its glories pass away;
Change and decay in all around I see;
O Thou who changest not, abide with me!

I need Thy presence ev'ry passing hour;
What but Thy grace can foil the tempter's pow'r?
Who like Thyself my guide and stay can be?
Through cloud and sunshine, O abide with me!

I fear no foe, with Thee at hand to bless;
Ills have no weight, and tears no bitterness.
Where is death's sting? where, grave, thy victory?
I triumph still, if Thou abide with me!

Hold Thou Thy cross before my closing eyes;
Shine through the gloom, and point me to the skies.
Heav'n's morning breaks, and earth's vain shadows
   flee —
In life, in death, O Lord, abide with me!

Again, these lines often comfort me:

> For ever with the Lord!
> Amen; so let it be;
> Life from the dead is in that word,
> 'Tis immortality.
> Here in the body pent,
> Absent from Him I roam,
> Yet nightly pitch my moving tent,
> A day's march nearer home.

And I have often been comforted to read these words:

> One sweetly solemn thought
> Comes to me o'er and o'er,
> I am nearer home today
> Than e'er I've been before.
>
> Nearer my Father's house,
> Where the many mansions be;
> Nearer the great white throne;
> Nearer the crystal sea;
>
> Nearer the bound of life,
> Where we lay our burdens down;
> Nearer leaving the cross;
> Nearer gaining the crown.

I am sure many of us have been greatly blessed when we read these words of Alfred Lord Tennyson,

> Sunset and evening star,
> And one clear call for me,
> And may there be no moaning of the bar
> When I put out to sea.
>
> But such a tide as moving seems asleep,
> Too full for sound or foam,
> When that which drew from out the boundless deep,
> Turns again home.
>
> Twilight and evening bell,
> And after that the dark,
> And may there be no sadness of farewell,
> When I embark.
>
> For though from out our bourne of time and place
> The flood may bear me far;
> I hope to see my Pilot face to face,
> When I have crossed the bar.

And so, we put our trust in the Lord. He is ours and we are His, and let me say to all who believe: "Look up." Look into His face and the nearer you come to that time of passing into His presence, the brighter it will be.

Aids
for
Consolation

THE LORD IS MY SHEPHERD

The Lord is my shepherd; I shall not
    want.
He maketh me to lie down in green pas-
    tures:
he leadeth me beside the still waters.
He restoreth my soul:
he leadeth me in the paths of righteous-
    ness for his name's sake.

Yea, though I walk through the valley of
    the shadow of death,
I will fear no evil: for thou art with me;
thy rod and thy staff they comfort me.

Thou preparest a table before me in the
    presence of mine enemies:
thou anointest my head with oil;
my cup runneth over.
Surely goodness and mercy shall follow me
    all the days of my life:
and I will dwell in the house of the Lord
    for ever.

—Psalm 23

THE LORD IS MY LIGHT AND MY SALVATION

The Lord is my light and my salvation;
    whom shall I fear?
The Lord is the strength of my life:
    of whom shall I be afraid?

When the wicked, even mine enemies and
    my foes,
came upon me to eat up my flesh,
they stumbled and fell.

Though a host should encamp against me,
my heart shall not fear:
though war should rise against me,
in this will I be confident.

One thing have I desired of the Lord,
that will I seek after;
that I may dwell in the house of the Lord
all the days of my life,
to behold the beauty of the Lord,
and to inquire in his temple.

For in the time of trouble he shall hide
    me in his pavilion:
in the secret of his tabernacle shall he hide
    me;
he shall set me up upon a rock.

And now shall mine head be lifted up
above mine enemies round about me:
therefore will I offer in his tabernacle
    sacrifices of joy;
I will sing, yea, I will sing praises unto the
    Lord.

Hear, O Lord, when I cry with my voice:
have mercy also upon me, and answer me.
When thou saidst, Seek ye my face;
my heart said unto thee,
Thy face, Lord, will I seek.

Hide not thy face far from me;
put not thy servant away in anger:
thou hast been my help;
leave me not, neither forsake me,
O God of my salvation.

When my father and my mother forsake me,
then the Lord will take me up.

Teach me thy way, O Lord,
and lead me in a plain path,
because of mine enemies.
Deliver me not over unto the will of mine
      enemies:
for false witnesses are risen up against me,
and such as breathe out cruelty.

I had fainted, unless I had believed
to see the goodness of the Lord in the land
      of the living.
Wait on the Lord:
be of good courage, and he shall strengthen
      thine heart:
wait, I say, on the Lord.

—Psalm 27

LORD, MAKE ME TO KNOW MINE END

Lord, make me to know mine end,
and the measure of my days, what it is;
that I may know how frail I am.
Behold, thou hast made my days as a hand-
      breadth;
and mine age is as nothing before thee:
verily every man at his best state is alto-
      gether vanity.
Surely every man walketh in a vain show;
surely they are disquieted in vain:
he heapeth up riches, and knoweth not who
      shall gather them.

And now, Lord, what wait I for?
My hope is in thee.
Deliver me from all my transgressions:
make me not the reproach of the foolish.
I was dumb, I opened not my mouth;
because thou didst it.
Remove thy stroke away from me:
I am consumed by the blow of thine hand.
When thou with rebukes dost correct man
    for iniquity,
thou makest his beauty to consume away
    like a moth:
surely every man is vanity.

Hear my prayer, O Lord, and give ear unto
    my cry;
hold not thy peace at my tears:
for I am a stranger with thee,
and a sojourner, as all my fathers were.
O spare me, that I may recover strength,
before I go hence, and be no more.
                    —Psalm 39:4-13

GOD IS OUR REFUGE AND STRENGTH

God is our refuge and strength,
a very present help in trouble.
Therefore will not we fear,
though the earth be removed,
and though the mountains be carried
into the midst of the sea;
though the waters thereof roar and be
    troubled,
though the mountains shake with the swell-
    ing thereof.

There is a river, the streams whereof shall
    make glad the city of God,
the holy place of the tabernacles of the
    Most High.
God is in the midst of her;
she shall not be moved:

God shall help her, and that right early.
The heathen raged, the kingdoms were
    moved:
he uttered his voice, the earth melted.
The Lord of hosts is with us;
the God of Jacob is our refuge.

Come, behold the works of the Lord,
what desolations he hath made in the earth.
He maketh wars to cease unto the end of
    the earth;
he breaketh the bow, and cutteth the spear
    in sunder;
he burneth the chariot in the fire.
Be still, and know that I am God:
I will be exalted among the heathen,
I will be exalted in the earth.
The Lord of hosts is with us;
the God of Jacob is our refuge.
                              —Psalm 46

LORD, THOU HAST BEEN OUR DWELLING PLACE

Lord, thou hast been our dwelling place
    in all generations.
Before the mountains were brought forth,
or ever thou hadst formed the earth and
    the world,
even from everlasting to everlasting, thou
    art God.

Thou turnest man to destruction;
and sayest, Return, ye children of men.
For a thousand years in thy sight
are but as yesterday when it is past,
and as a watch in the night.

Thou carriest them away as with a flood;
    they are as a sleep:
in the morning they are like grass which
    groweth up.
In the morning it flourisheth, and groweth
    up;
in the evening it is cut down, and withereth.

For we are consumed by thine anger,
and by thy wrath are we troubled.
Thou hast set our iniquities before thee,
our secret sins in the light of thy countenance.

For all our days are passed away in thy
    wrath;
we spend our years as a tale that is told.
The days of our years are threescore years
    and ten;
and if by reason of strength they be four-
    score years,
yet is their strength labor and sorrow;
for it is soon cut off, and we fly away.

Who knoweth the power of thine anger?
Even according to thy fear, so is thy wrath.
So teach us to number our days,
that we may apply our hearts unto wisdom.
                      —Psalm 90:1-12

LIKE AS A FATHER PITIETH HIS CHILDREN

Like as a father pitieth his children,
so the Lord pitieth them that fear him.
For he knoweth our frame;
he remembereth that we are dust.
As for man, his days are as grass:
as a flower of the field, so he flourisheth.
For the wind passeth over it, and it is gone;
and the place thereof shall know it no
        more.
But the mercy of the Lord is from ever-
        lasting to everlasting
upon them that fear him,
and his righteousness unto children's children:
to such as keep his covenant,
and to those that remember his command-
        ments to do them.
                      —Psalm 103:13-18

I WILL LIFT UP MINE EYES UNTO THE HILLS

I will lift up mine eyes unto the hills,
from whence cometh my help.
My help cometh from the Lord,
which made heaven and earth.

He will not suffer thy foot to be moved:
he that keepeth thee will not slumber.
Behold, he that keepeth Israel
shall neither slumber nor sleep.

The Lord is thy keeper:
the Lord is thy shade upon thy right
    hand.
The sun shall not smite thee by day,
nor the moon by night.

The Lord shall preserve thee from all evil:
he shall preserve thy soul.
The Lord shall preserve thy going out and
    thy coming in
from this time forth, and even for ever-
    more.

—Psalm 121

OUT OF THE DEPTHS HAVE I CRIED
UNTO THEE, O LORD

Out of the depths have I cried unto thee,
    O Lord.
Lord, hear my voice:
let thine ears be attentive
to the voice of my supplications.

If thou, Lord, shouldest mark iniquities,
O Lord, who shall stand?
But there is forgiveness with thee,
that thou mayest be feared.

I wait for the Lord,
my soul doth wait,
and in his word do I hope.
My soul waiteth for the Lord
more than they that watch for the morning:
I say, more than they that watch for the
    morning.

Let Israel hope in the Lord:
for with the Lord there is mercy,
and with him is plenteous redemption.
And he shall redeem Israel
from all his iniquities.
—Psalm 130

REMEMBER NOW THY CREATOR

Remember now thy Creator in the days of thy youth, while the evil days come not, nor the years draw nigh, when thou shalt say, I have no pleasure in them; while the sun, or the light, or the moon, or the stars, be not darkened, nor the clouds return after the rain: in the day when the keepers of the house shall tremble, and the strong men shall bow themselves, and the grinders cease because they are few, and those that look out of the windows be darkened, and the doors shall be shut in the streets, when the sound of the grinding is low, and he shall rise up at the voice of the bird, and all the daughters of music shall be brought low; also when they shall be afraid of that which is high, and fears shall be in the way, and the almond tree shall flourish, and the grasshopper shall be a burden, and desire shall fail: because man goeth to his long home, and the mourners go about the streets: or ever the silver cord be loosed, or the golden bowl be broken, or the pitcher be broken at the fountain, or the wheel broken at the cistern. Then shall the dust return to the earth as it was: and the spirit shall return unto God who gave it. Vanity of vanities, saith the preacher; all is vanity.

And moreover, because the preacher was wise, he still taught the people knowledge; yea, he gave good heed, and sought out, and set in order many proverbs. The preacher sought to find out acceptable words: and that which was written was upright, even words of truth. The words of the wise are as goads, and as nails fastened by the masters of assemblies, which are given from one shepherd. And further, by these, my son, be admonished: of making many books there is no end; and much study is a weariness of the flesh. Let us hear the conclusion of the whole matter: Fear God, and keep his commandments: for this is the whole duty of man. For God shall bring every work into judgment, with every secret thing, whether it be good, or whether it be evil.
—Ecclesiastes 12

HAST THOU NOT KNOWN?

Hast thou not known? hast thou not heard, that the everlasting God, the Lord, the Creator of the ends of the

earth, fainteth not, neither is weary? there is no search-
ing of his understanding. He giveth power to the faint;
and to them that have no might he increaseth strength.
Even the youths shall faint and be weary, and the young
men shall utterly fall: but they that wait upon the Lord
shall renew their strength; they shall mount up with
wings as eagles; they shall run, and not be weary; and
they shall walk, and not faint.
—Isaiah 40:28-31

FEAR NOT: FOR I HAVE REDEEMED THEE

But now thus saith the Lord that created thee, O
Jacob, and he that formed thee, O Israel, Fear not: for I
have redeemed thee, I have called thee by thy name;
thou art mine. When thou passest through the waters, I
will be with thee; and through the rivers, they shall not
overflow thee: when thou walkest through the fire, thou
shalt not be burned; neither shall the flame kindle upon
thee. For I am the Lord thy God, the Holy One of Israel,
thy Saviour; I gave Egypt for thy ransom, Ethiopia and
Seba for thee.
—Isaiah 43:1-3

HE IS NOT HERE, HE IS RISEN

And they entered in, and found not the body of the
Lord Jesus. And it came to pass, as they were much per-
plexed thereabout, behold, two men stood by them in
shining garments: and as they were afraid, and bowed
down their faces to the earth, they said unto them, Why
seek ye the living among the dead? He is not here, but is
risen: remember how he spake unto you when he was
yet in Galilee, saying, The Son of man must be delivered
into the hands of sinful men, and be crucified, and the
third day rise again. And they remembered his words.
—Luke 24:3-8

THY BROTHER SHALL RISE AGAIN

Then said Martha unto Jesus, Lord, if thou hadst been
here, my brother had not died. But I know, that even
now, whatsoever thou wilt ask of God, God will give it
thee. Jesus saith unto her, Thy brother shall rise again.
Martha saith unto him, I know that he shall rise again in

the resurrection at the last day. Jesus said unto her, I am the resurrection, and the life: he that believeth in me, though he were dead, yet shall he live: and whosoever liveth and believeth in me shall never die. Believest thou this?

—John 11:21-26

LET NOT YOUR HEART BE TROUBLED

Let not your heart be troubled: ye believe in God, believe also in me. In my Father's house are many mansions: if it were not so, I would have told you. I go to prepare a place for you. And if I go and prepare a place for you, I will come again, and receive you unto myself; that where I am, there ye may be also. And whither I go ye know, and the way ye know. Thomas saith unto him, Lord, we know not whither thou goest; and how can we know the way? Jesus saith unto him, I am the way, the truth, and the life: no man cometh unto the Father, but by me.

—John 14:1-6

AS MANY AS ARE LED BY THE SPIRIT OF GOD

For as many as are led by the Spirit of God, they are the sons of God. For ye have not received the spirit of bondage again to fear; but ye have received the Spirit of adoption, whereby we cry, Abba, Father. The Spirit itself beareth witness with our spirit, that we are the children of God: and if children, then heirs; heirs of God, and joint-heirs with Christ; if so be that we suffer with him, that we may be also glorified together. For I reckon that the sufferings of this present time are not worthy to be compared with the glory which shall be revealed in us. For the earnest expectation of the creature waiteth for the manifestation of the sons of God. For the creature was made subject to vanity, not willingly, but by reason of him who hath subjected the same in hope. Because the creature itself also shall be delivered from the bondage of corruption into the glorious liberty of the children of God. For we know that the whole creation groaneth and travaileth in pain together until now. And not only they, but ourselves also, which have the first fruits of the Spirit, even we ourselves groan within ourselves, waiting for the adoption, to wit, the redemption of our body. For we are saved by hope: but hope that is seen is not hope: for what a man seeth, why doth he yet hope for? But if we hope for that we see not, then do we with patience wait for it. Likewise the Spirit also helpeth our infirmities: for we know not what we should pray for as we ought: but the spirit itself maketh intercession for us with groanings which cannot be uttered. And he that searcheth the hearts knoweth what is the mind of the Spirit, because he maketh intercession for the saints according to the will of God. And we know that all things work together for good to them that love God, to them who are the called according to his purpose. For whom he did foreknow, he also did predestinate to be conformed to the image of his Son, that he might be the first-born among many brethren. Moreover whom he did predestinate, them he also called: and whom he called, them he also justified: and whom he justified, them he also glorified. What shall we then say to these things? If God be for us, who can be against us? He that spared not his own Son, but delivered him up for us all, how shall he not with him also freely give us all things? Who shall lay any thing to the charge of God's elect? It is God that justifieth. Who is he that condemneth? It is Christ that died, yea rather, that is risen again, who is even at the right hand of God, who also maketh intercession for us. Who shall separate us from the love of Christ? shall tribulation, or distress, or persecution, or famine, or nakedness, or peril, or sword? As it is written, For thy sake we are killed all the day long; we are accounted as sheep for the slaughter. Nay, in all these things we are more than conquerors through him that loved us. For I am persuaded, that neither death, nor life, nor angels, nor principalities, nor powers, nor things present, nor things to come, nor height, nor depth, nor any other creature, shall be able to separate us from the love of God, which is in Christ Jesus our Lord.

—Romans 8:14-39

NOW IS CHRIST RISEN FROM THE DEAD

But now is Christ risen from the dead, and become the first fruits of them that slept. For since by man came death, by man came also the resurrection of the dead.

For as in Adam all die, even so in Christ shall all be made alive. But every man in his own order: Christ the first fruits; afterwards they that are Christ's at his coming. Then cometh the end, when he shall have delivered up the kingdom to God, even the Father; when he shall have put down all rule and all authority and power. For he must reign, till he hath put all enemies under his feet. The last enemy that shall be destroyed is death. For he hath put all things under his feet. But when he saith all things are put under him, it is manifest that he is excepted, which did put all things under him. And when all things shall be subdued unto him, then shall the Son also himself be subject unto him that put all things under him, that God may be all in all. Else what shall they do which are baptized for the dead, if the dead rise not at all? why are they then baptized for the dead? And why stand we in jeopardy every hour? I protest by your rejoicing which I have in Christ Jesus our Lord, I die daily. If after the manner of men I have fought with beasts at Ephesus, what advantageth it me, if the dead rise not? let us eat and drink; for tomorrow we die. Be not deceived: evil communications corrupt good manners. Awake to righteousness, and sin not; for some have not the knowledge of God: I speak this to your shame. But some man will say, How are the dead raised up? and with what body do they come? Thou fool, that which thou sowest is not quickened, except it die: and that which thou sowest, thou sowest not that body that shall be, but bare grain, it may chance of wheat, or of some other grain: but God giveth it a body as it hath pleased him, and to every seed his own body. All flesh is not the same flesh: but there is one kind of flesh of men, another flesh of beasts, another of fishes, and another of birds. There are also celestial bodies, and bodies terrestrial: but the glory of the celestial is one, and the glory of the terrestrial is another. There is one glory of the sun, and another glory of the moon, and another glory of the stars: for one star differeth from another star in glory. So also is the resurrection of the dead. It is sown in corruption; it is raised in incorruption: it is sown in dishonor; it is raised in glory: it is sown in weakness; it is raised in power: it is sown a natural body; it is raised a spiritual body. There is a natural body, and there is a spiritual body. And so it is written, The first man Adam

was made a living soul; the last Adam was made a quickening spirit. Howbeit that was not first which is spiritual, but that which is natural; and afterward that which is spiritual. The first man is of the earth, earthy: the second man is the Lord from heaven. As is the earthy, such are they also that are earthy: and as is the heavenly, such are they also that are heavenly. And as we have borne the image of the earthy, we shall also bear the image of the heavenly. Now this I say, brethren, that flesh and blood cannot inherit the kingdom of God; neither doth corruption inherit incorruption. Behold, I show you a mystery; We shall not all sleep, but we shall all be changed, in a moment, in the twinkling of an eye, at the last trump: for the trumpet shall sound, and the dead shall be raised incorruptible, and we shall be changed. For this corruptible must put on incorruption, and this mortal must put on immortality. So when this corruptible shall have put on incorruption, and this mortal shall have put on immortality, then shall be brought to pass the saying that is written, Death is swallowed up in victory. O death, where is thy sting? O grave, where is thy victory? The sting of death is sin; and the strength of sin is the law. But thanks be to God, which giveth us the victory through our Lord Jesus Christ. Therefore, my beloved brethren, be ye steadfast, unmovable, always abounding in the work of the Lord, forasmuch as ye know that your labor is not in vain in the Lord.
—I Corinthians 15:20-58

DESIRE TO DEPART

For I am in a strait betwixt two, having a desire to depart, and to be with Christ; which is far better.
—Philippians 1:23

CONCERNING THEM WHICH ARE ASLEEP

But I would not have you to be ignorant, brethren, concerning them which are asleep, that ye sorrow not, even as others which have no hope. For if we believe that Jesus died and rose again, even so them also which sleep in Jesus will God bring with him. For this we say unto you by the word of the Lord, that we which are alive and remain unto the coming of the Lord shall not prevent them which are asleep. For the Lord himself shall descend from heaven with a shout, with the voice of the archangel, and with the trump of God: and the dead in Christ shall rise first: then we which are alive and remain shall be caught up together with them in the clouds, to meet the Lord in the air: and so shall we ever be with the Lord. Wherefore comfort one another with these words.

—I Thessalonians 4:13-18

THEREFORE ARE THEY BEFORE THE THRONE OF GOD

Therefore are they before the throne of God, and serve him day and night in his temple: and he that sitteth on the throne shall dwell among them. They shall hunger no more, neither thirst any more; neither shall the sun light on them, nor any heat. For the Lamb which is in the midst of the throne shall feed them, and shall lead them unto living fountains of waters: and God shall wipe away all tears from their eyes.

—Revelation 7:15-17

BLESSED ARE THE DEAD WHICH DIE IN THE LORD

And I heard a voice from heaven saying unto me, Write, Blessed are the dead which die in the Lord from henceforth: Yea, saith the Spirit, that they may rest from their labors; and their works do follow them.

—Revelation 14:13

AND GOD SHALL WIPE AWAY ALL TEARS FROM THEIR EYES

And I heard a great voice out of heaven saying, Behold, the tabernacle of God is with men, and he will dwell with them, and they shall be his people, and God himself shall be with them, and be their God. And God shall wipe away all tears from their eyes; and there shall be no more death, neither sorrow, nor crying, neither shall there be any more pain: for the former things are passed away.

—Revelation 21:3-4

CALL IT NOT DEATH

Call it not death
When swift release from suffering and pain
Heralds a Kingdom free from ills:
A glorious reign.

Call it not death
When visions fair dispel this earthly night
And those things now but darkly seen
Become as light.

Call it not death
When heavenly hosts in radiant array
Welcome the liberated soul
To endless day.
—Sarah Bernstein Gutzke

ABIDE WITH ME

Abide with me; fast falls the eventide;
The darkness deepens; Lord, with me abide;
When other helpers fail, and comforts flee,
Help of the helpless, O abide with me.

Swift to its close ebbs out life's little day;
Earth's joys grow dim, its glories pass away;
Change and decay in all around I see;
O Thou, Who changest not, abide with me.

I need Thy presence every passing hour;
What but Thy grace can foil the tempter's power?
Who like Thyself my guide and stay can be?
Through cloud and sunshine, Lord, abide with me.

I fear no foe with Thee at hand to bless;
Ills have no weight, and tears no bitterness;
Where is death's sting? Where, Grave, thy victory?
I triumph still, if Thou abide with me.

Hold Thou Thy Cross before my closing eyes;
Shine through the gloom, and point me to the skies;
Heaven's morning breaks, and earth's vain shadows flee;
In life, in death, O Lord, abide with me.
—H. F. Lyte

LEAD, KINDLY LIGHT

Lead, kindly light, amid the encircling gloom,
    Lead Thou me on;
The night is dark, and I am far from home,
    Lead Thou me on.
Keep Thou my feet; I do not ask to see
The distant scene; one step enough for me.

I was not ever thus, nor prayed that Thou
    Shouldst lead me on;
I loved to choose and see my path; but now
    Lead Thou me on.
I loved the garish day, and, spite of fears,
Pride ruled my will: remember not past years.

So long Thy power hath blest me, sure it still
    Will lead me on,
O'er moor and fen, o'er crag and torrent, till
    The night is gone;
And with the morn those Angel faces smile,
Which I have loved long since, and lost awhile.
    —John Henry Newman

NOW THE LABOURER'S TASK IS O'ER

Now the labourer's task is o'er;
    Now the battle day is past;
Now upon the farther shore
    Lands the voyager at last.
Father, in Thy gracious keeping
Leave we now Thy servant sleeping.

There the tears of earth are dried;
    There its hidden things are clear;
There the work of life is tried
    By a juster judge than here.
Father, in Thy gracious keeping
Leave we now Thy servant sleeping.

There the sinful souls, that turn
    To the cross their dying eyes,
All the love of Christ shall learn
    At His feet in Paradise.
Father, in Thy gracious keeping
Leave we now Thy servant sleeping.

There no more the powers of hell
    Can prevail to mar their peace;
Christ the Lord shall guard them well,
    He Who died for their release.
Father, in Thy gracious keeping
Leave we now Thy servant sleeping.

"Earth to earth, and dust to dust,"
    Calmly now the words we say.
Leaving (him) to sleep in trust
    Till the Resurrection day.
Father, in Thy gracious keeping
Leave we now Thy servant sleeping.
—J. Ellerton

PEACE, PERFECT PEACE

Peace, perfect peace, in this dark world of sin?
The Blood of Jesus whispers peace within.

Peace, perfect peace, by thronging duties press'd?
To do the will of Jesus, this is rest.

Peace, perfect peace, with sorrows surging round?
On Jesus' bosom nought but calm is found.

Peace, perfect peace, with loved ones far away?
In Jesus' keeping we are safe and they.

Peace, perfect peace, our future all unknown?
Jesus we know, and He is on the throne.

Peace, perfect peace, death shadowing us and ours?
Jesus has vanquish'd death and all its powers.

It is enough: earth's struggles soon shall cease,
And Jesus call us to heav'n's perfect peace.
—E. H. Bickersteth

FOREVER WITH THE LORD

"For ever with the Lord!"
    Amen; so let it be;
Life from the dead is in that word,
    'Tis immortality.
Here in the body pent,
    Absent from Him I roam,
Yet nightly pitch my moving tent,
    A day's march nearer home.

My Father's house on high,
    Home of my soul, how near
At times to faith's foreseeing eye
    Thy golden gates appear!
Ah! then my spirit faints
    To reach the land I love,
The bright inheritance of saints,
    Jerusalem above.

"For ever with the Lord!"
    Father, if 'tis Thy will,
The promise of that faithful word
    Even here to me fulfil.
Be Thou at my right hand,
    Then can I never fail;
Uphold Thou me, and I shall stand,
    Fight, and I must prevail.

So when my latest breath
    Shall rend the veil in twain,
By death I shall escape from death,
    And life eternal gain.
Knowing as I am known,
    How shall I love that word,
And oft repeat before the throne,
    "For ever with the Lord!"
                    —J. Montgomery

GOOD-NIGHT

Sleep on beloved, sleep, and take thy rest;
Lay down thy head upon the Saviour's breast;
We loved thee well, but Jesus loved thee best,
    Good-night! Good-night! Good-night!

Calm is thy slumber as an infant's sleep,
But thou shalt wake no more to toil and weep,
Thine is a perfect rest, secure and deep;
    Good-night! Good-night! Good-night!

Until the shadows from the earth are cast,
Until he gathers in his sheaves at last,
Until the twilight gloom is overpast;
    Good-night! Good-night! Good-night!

Until the Easter glory lights the skies,
Until the dead in Jesus shall arise,
And he shall come, but not in lowly guise;
    Good-night! Good-night! Good-night!

Only good-night! beloved, not farewell,
A little while and all his sons shall dwell
In hallowed union indivisible.
    Good-night! Good-night! Good-night!

Until we meet again before his throne,
Clothed in the spotless robes he gives his own,
Until we know even as we are known,
    Good-night! Good-night! Good-night!
                —Sarah Doudney

JESUS, SAVIOUR, PILOT ME

Jesus, Saviour, pilot me
Over life's tempestuous sea;
Unknown waves before me roll,
Hiding rock and treach'rous shoal;
Chart and compass came from Thee:
Jesus, Saviour, pilot me.

As a mother stills her child,
Thou canst hush the ocean wild;
Boist'rous waves obey Thy will
When Thou say'st to them, "Be still."
Wond'rous Sov'reign of the sea,
Jesus, Saviour, pilot me.

When at last I near the shore,
And the fearful breakers roar
'Twixt me and the peaceful rest,
Then, while leaning on Thy breast,
May I hear Thee say to me,
"Fear not, I will pilot thee."
—Edward Hopper

ONE SWEETLY SOLEMN THOUGHT

One sweetly solemn thought
    Comes to me o'er and o'er,
I am nearer home to-day
    Than e'er I've been before.

Nearer my Father's house,
    Where the many mansions be;
Nearer the great white throne;
    Nearer the crystal sea;

Nearer the bound of life,
    Where we lay our burdens down;
Nearer leaving the cross;
    Nearer gaining the crown.

But the waves of that silent sea
    Roll dark before my sight,
That brightly on the other side
    Break on a shore of light.

O if my mortal feet
    Have almost gained the brink,
If it be I am nearer home
    Even today than I think,

Father, perfect my trust;
    Let my spirit feel in death
That her feet are firmly set
    On the rock of a living faith.
                    —Phoebe Cary

IT IS NOT DEATH TO DIE

It is not death to die—
    To leave this weary road,
And, 'midst the brotherhood on high,
    To be at home with God.

It is not death to close
    The eye long dimmed with tears,
And wake in glorious repose
    To spend eternal years.

It is not death to bear
    The wrench that sets us free
From dungeon chain, to breathe the air
    Of boundless liberty.

It is not death to fling
    Aside this sinful dust,
And rise on strong exulting wing
    To live among the just.

Jesus, Thou Prince of Life,
    Thy chosen cannot die;
Like Thee, they conquer in the strife,
    To reign with Thee on high.
                    —H. A. Cesar Malan,
                Tr. George Washington Bethune

IN MY FATHER'S HOUSE

No, not cold beneath the grasses,
Not close-walled within the tomb;
Rather, in our Father's mansion,
Living in another room.

Living, like the man who loves me,
Like my child with cheeks abloom,
Out of sight, at desk or school-book,
Busy in another room.

Nearer than my son whom fortune
Beckons where the strange lands loom;
Just behind the hanging curtain,
Serving in another room.

Shall I doubt my Father's mercy?
Shall I think of death as doom,
Or the stepping o'er the threshold
To a bigger, brighter room?

Shall I blame my Father's wisdom?
Shall I sit enswathed in gloom,
When I know my loves are happy—
Waiting, in another room?
—Robert Freeman

CROSSING THE BAR

Sunset and evening star,
And one clear call for me,
And may there be no moaning of the bar
When I put out to sea.

But such a tide as moving seems asleep,
Too full for sound or foam,
When that which drew from out the boundless deep,
Turns again home.

Twilight and evening bell,
And after that the dark,
And may there be no sadness of farewell,
When I embark.

For though from out our bourne of time and place
The flood may bear me far;
I hope to see my Pilot face to face,
When I have crossed the bar.
—Alfred Lord Tennyson

HE GIVETH HIS BELOVED SLEEP

Of all the thoughts of God that are
Borne inward unto souls afar,
Along the Psalmist's music deep,
Now tell me if there any is
For gift or grace surpassing this,
    "He giveth His beloved sleep."

And friends! dear friends! when it shall be
That this low breath is gone from me,
And round my bier you come to weep,
Let one, most loving of you all,
Say, "Not a tear must o'er him fall" —
    "He giveth His beloved sleep."
                    —Elizabeth Barrett Browning

WHEN EARTH'S LAST PICTURE IS PAINTED

When earth's last picture is painted
    And the tubes are twisted and dried,
When the oldest colors have faded,
    And the youngest critic has died.
We shall rest—and faith, we shall need it—
    Lie down for an aeon or two,
Till the Master of all Good Workmen
    Shall set us to work anew!

And those who are good shall be happy;
    They shall sit in a golden chair;
They shall splash at a ten-league canvas
    With brushes of comet's hair;
They shall find real saints to draw from,
    Magdalene, Peter and Paul:
They shall work for an age at a sitting
    And never grow weary at all!

And only the Master shall praise them,
    And only the Master shall blame,
And no one shall work for money,
    And no one shall work for fame,
But each for the joy of the working,
    And each in his separate star
Shall draw the thing as he sees it,
    For the God of things as they are.
                    —Rudyard Kipling

COMFORT

There is a day of sunny rest
        For every dark and troubled night;
And grief may bide an evening guest,
        But joy shall come with early light.

For God hath marked each sorrowing day,
        And numbered every secret tear,
And heaven's long age of bliss shall pay
        For all His children suffer here.
                        —William Cullen Bryant

From THANATOPSIS

So live that when thy summons comes to join
The innumerable caravan, which moves
To that mysterious realm, where each shall take
His chamber in the silent halls of death,
Thou go not, like the quarry-slave at night,
Scourged to his dungeon, but, sustained and soothed
By an unfaltering trust, approach thy grave
Like one who wraps the drapery of his couch
About him, and lies down to pleasant dreams.
                —William Cullen Bryant